Wildfire Damages to Homes and Resources: Understanding Causes and Reducing Losses

Kelsi Bracmort
Specialist in Agricultural Conservation and Natural Resources Policy

March 12, 2012

Congressional Research Service

7-5700

www.crs.gov

RL34517

Summary

Wildfires are getting more severe, with more acres and houses burned and more people at risk. This results from excess biomass in the forests, due to past logging and grazing and a century of fire suppression, combined with an expanding wildland-urban interface—more people and houses in and near the forests—and climate change, exacerbating drought and insect and disease problems. Some assert that current efforts to protect houses and to reduce biomass (through fuel treatments, such as thinning) are inadequate, and that public objections to some of these activities on federal lands raise costs and delay action. Others counter that proposals for federal lands allow timber harvesting with substantial environmental damage and little fire protection. Congress is addressing these issues through various legislative proposals and through funding for protection programs.

Wildfires are inevitable—biomass, dry conditions, and lightning create fires. Some are *surface fires*, which burn needles, grasses, and other fine fuels and leave most trees alive. Others are *crown fires*, which are typically driven by high winds and burn biomass at all levels from the ground through the tree tops. Many wildfires contain areas of both surface and crown fires. Surface fires are relatively easy to control, but crown fires are difficult, if not impossible, to stop; often, crown fires burn until they run out of fuel or the weather changes.

Homes can be ignited by direct contact with fire, by radiative heating, and by *firebrands* (burning materials lifted by the wind or the fire's own convection column). Protection of homes must address all three. Research has identified the keys to protecting structures: having a non-flammable roof; clearing burnable materials that abut the house (e.g., plants, flammable mulch, woodpiles, wooden decks); and landscaping to create a defensible space around the structure.

Wildland and resource damages from fire vary widely, depending on the nature of the ecosystem as well as on site-specific conditions. Surface fire ecosystems, which burn on 5- to 35-year cycles, can be damaged by crown fires due to unnatural fuel accumulations and *fuel ladders* (small trees and dense undergrowth); fuel treatments probably prevent some crown fires in such ecosystems. Stand-replacement fire ecosystems are those where crown fires are natural and the species are adapted to periodic crown fires; fuel treatments are unlikely to alter the historic fire regime of such ecosystems. In mixed-intensity fire ecosystems, where a mix of surface and crown fires is historically normal, it is unclear whether fuel treatments would alter wildfire patterns.

Prescribed burning (intentional fires) and mechanical treatments (cutting and removing some trees) can reduce resource damages caused by wildfires in some ecosystems. However, prescribed fires are risky, mechanical treatments can cause other ecological damages, and both are expensive. Proponents of more treatment advocate expedited processes for environmental and public review of projects to hasten action and cut costs, but others caution that inadequate review can allow unintended damages with few fire protection benefits.

Contents

Tables

Appendixes

Contacts

Wildfires have been getting more severe in recent fire seasons; the 2004, 2005, 2006, 2007, and 2011 seasons were the most severe since 1960.[1] An escaped prescribed fire that burned 239 houses in Los Alamos, NM, in May 2000 focused national attention on the growing wildfire problem. The fire in Los Alamos highlighted the *wildland-urban interface* problem.[2] At that time, 2000 was the second most severe fire season since 1960, eclipsed only by the 1988 Yellowstone fires.[3] President Clinton responded with a new National Fire Plan to increase funding for wildfire protection.

It has been widely proclaimed that the increasing severity of wildfires is a result of excessive biomass accumulations. In at least some ecosystems, logging, livestock grazing, and a century of fire suppression efforts have allowed biomass fuels to accumulate to unnatural levels. Climate change, and its impacts on drought, fire, and insects and diseases, could exacerbate these problems. Many interests have proposed fuel reduction treatments as a means to lower the fuel levels and thus reduce the wildfire threat to homes and to wildlands. The severe 2002 fire season led President Bush to propose a Healthy Forests Initiative to expedite efforts to reduce biomass fuels on federal lands, and in 2003, Congress enacted the Healthy Forests Restoration Act to expedite federal fuel reduction and other forest protection programs.

Some interests are concerned that current efforts to reduce fuel levels on federal lands are inadequate, and that "environmentalist objections" to some of those efforts are unnecessarily raising costs and delaying action. Others counter that some efforts are so broad that they permit substantial timber sales without significantly reducing wildfire risks for communities. Congress continues to address these issues as it considers funding and legislative proposals.

This report focuses on options for protecting structures and for protecting wildlands and natural resources from wildfires. It begins with a brief overview of the nature of wildfires, followed by a discussion of protecting structures. Then, it discusses wildfire damages to wildlands and natural resources, fuel treatment options and their benefits and limitations, and public involvement in federal decisions.

Background: Fires Happen

In temperate ecosystems, wildfires are inevitable. The combination of biomass plus dry conditions—in the short term (e.g., the annual dry season) or in the long term (e.g., drought or climate change)—equals fuel to burn. Add an ignition source, such as lightning, and wildfire happens. Fire is a self-sustaining chemical reaction that perpetuates itself as long as all three

---

[1] National Interagency Fire Center, "Total Wildland Fires and Acres," at http://www.nifc.gov/fireInfo/ fireInfo_stats_totalFires.html. Fire season severity is commonly assessed by acres burned, but larger fires may not be "worse" if they burn less intensely, because their damages may be lower. However, fire intensity and damages are not measured for each wildfire, and thus cannot be used to gauge the severity of fire seasons. It is unclear whether acreage burned might be a reasonable approximation of severity.

[2] The wildland-urban interface is an area where structures (usually homes) are in or near wildlands (forests or rangelands). For more information, see CRS Report RS21880, *Wildfire Protection in the Wildland-Urban Interface*, by Ross W. Gorte and Kelsi Bracmort.

[3] Subsequent fire seasons have surpassed the 2000 season, while the 1988 data have been revised downward.

elements of the fire triangle—fuel, heat, and oxygen—remain available. Fire control focuses on removing one of those elements.

There are two principal kinds of wildfire, although an individual wildfire may contain areas of both kinds.[4] One is a *surface fire*, which burns the needles or leaves, grass, and other small biomass within a foot or so of the ground and quickly moves on. Such fires are relatively easy to control by removing fuel with a *fireline*, essentially a dirt path wide enough to eliminate the continuous fuels needed to sustain the fire, or by cooling or smothering the flames with water or dirt.

The other principal kind of wildfire is a *crown fire*, also called a conflagration. Crown fires burn biomass at all levels—from the surface through the tops of the crowns of the trees—although they do not consume all the biomass; logs and large limbs may need to burn for hours before being completely reduced to ashes. Rather, a crown fire quickly burns the needles or leaves and small twigs and limbs on the surface and throughout the crown of the trees. Because the needles and leaves in the crown are green, they require more energy to burn than dry fuels on the surface. Furthermore, because of the green fuels and the often discontinuous biomass of the canopy, wind is usually needed to sustain a crown fire. Once burning vigorously, a crown fire can create its own wind (the strong upward convection of the heated air can draw in cooler air from surrounding areas, thus creating a wind that feeds the fire). The strong upward convection can also lift burning biomass (*firebrands*) and send it soaring ahead of the fire, creating spot fires and accelerating the spread of the wildfire. Crown fires typically include areas of surface fire and unburned areas within their perimeters.

Not surprisingly, crown fires are difficult, if not impossible, to control. Unless quite wide, firelines may be ineffective to control crown fires, especially if winds are causing spot fires. Water or fire retardant (*slurry*) dropped from helicopters or airplanes can sometimes knock a crown fire down (back to a surface fire) if the area burning and the winds are not too great. Often, however, crown fires burn until they run out of fuel or the weather changes (the wind dies or it rains or snows).

Nearly all fires are "patchy," with a mix of areas of varying fire severities, depending on site-specific fuel, moisture, and wind conditions. This patchiness makes understanding and controlling wildfires difficult at best.

Protecting Structures from Wildfires

Wildfires occasionally burn houses, in a zone commonly called the *wildland-urban interface*.[5] In recent years, it seems one or more fires annually have burned down several to a few hundred homes and outbuildings (sheds, garages, etc.). These structures generally have ignited in one of three ways: through direct contact with fire, through radiation (heating from exposure to flames),

---

[4] See Stephen F. Arno and Steven Allison-Bunnell, *Flames in Our Forest: Disaster or Renewal?* (Washington, DC: Island Press, 2002), pp. 45-46.

[5] For information on the interface, see CRS Report RS21880, *Wildfire Protection in the Wildland-Urban Interface*, by Ross W. Gorte and Kelsi Bracmort.

and through firebrands.[6] The likelihood of a structure burning from one of these ignition methods is called *home ignitability*.[7]

Home Ignitability

Research has identified three essential elements to protecting structures: the roof; adjacent burnable materials; and the landscaping. Treating these three elements addresses all three ways by which structures are ignited—direct contact, radiation, and firebrands.

The roof is critical to protecting structures from wildfires.[8] Firebrands that land on a flammable roof can ignite the roof. Untreated red cedar shakes and shingles are particularly problematic: "A major cause of home loss in wildland areas is flammable woodshake roofs."[9] Fire retardant treatments are sufficient for wood shakes, but the effectiveness of such treatments degrades over time.[10] Alternatives include tile, slate, metals (e.g., copper or aluminum), and other non-flammable materials. Walls, doors and windows, and vents can also contribute to the protection, or destruction, of a structure, depending on materials, location, and other variables.[11]

Adjacent burnable materials are items that can burn that abut the house. This can include plants (live or dead) and flammable mulch (e.g., wood chips or bark) under an overhang or eave or next to the structure, gutters clogged with leaves or needles, decks and porches, sheds and garages, and especially woodpiles. These factors were particularly important for the 239 homes burned by the Cerro Grande fire in Los Alamos, NM, in May 2000: "The high ignitability of Los Alamos was principally due to the abundance and ubiquity of pine needles, dead leaves, cured vegetation, flammable shrubs, and wood piles that were adjacent to, touching, or covering parts of homes."[12] One source recommended that "when assessing the ignition potential of a structure, attachments [such as decks, porches, and fences] are considered part of the structure."[13]

Finally, landscaping—the character of the vegetation surrounding the house—is critical to preventing both direct burning and ignition by radiation. Recommended *defensible space* around structures is at least 30 feet or 10 meters, with greater distances for steeper slopes (because of up-slope convection heating) and for larger vegetation (least for grass, more for shrubs, most for mature forest).[14] Others recommend greater distances, such as 100 feet.[15] One researcher

---

[6] National Wildland/Urban Interface, Fire Protection Program, *Wildland/Urban Interface Fire Hazard Assessment Methodology*, p. 5, at http://www.firewise.org/resources/files/wham.pdf.

[7] Jack D. Cohen, "Preventing Disaster: Home Ignitability in the Wildland-Urban Interface," *Journal of Forestry* (March 2000), p. 17.

[8] *FireSmart: Protecting Your Community From Wildfire* (Edmonton, Alberta: Partners in Protection, May 1999), pp. 2-5.

[9] *Wildland/Urban Interface Fire Hazard Assessment Methodology*, p. 7.

[10] *Is Your Home Protected From Wildfire Disaster? A Homeowner's Guide to Wildfire Retrofit* (Tampa, FL: Institute for Business and Home Safety, n.d.), p. 9, at http://www.firewise.org/resources/files/wildfr2.pdf.

[11] *Wildland/Urban Interface Fire Hazard Assessment Methodology*, p. 7.

[12] Jack Cohen, "The Cerro Grande Fire: Why Houses Burned," *Forest Trust Quarterly Report*, no. 23 (Dec. 2000), p. 7.

[13] *Wildland/Urban Interface Fire Hazard Assessment Methodology*, p. 7.

[14] *FireSmart*, pp. 2-11, and Robert Bardon and Robin Carter, *Minimizing Wildfire Risk—A Forest Landowner's Guide*, 03/03-30M-DSB/SSS AG-616 (North Carolina Cooperative Extension Service, n.d.), p. 6.

---

calculated that the ignition time for an untreated wood wall was more than 10 minutes at a distance of 40 meters (about 130 feet).[16] With burning durations for crown fires "on the order of 1 minute at a specific location," the "safe distance" for an untreated wood wall was calculated to be 27 meters (less than 90 feet), which is consistent with field tests documenting wall ignition times for experimental crown fires in Canada.[17] The same source notes older fire case studies documenting structure survival—95% survival for 10-18 meter (about 32-60 feet) clearance in the 1961 Belair-Brentwood (CA) fire and 86% survival for 10+ meter clearance in the 1990 Painted Cave (CA) fire.[18] Thus, clearing to 40 meters would likely be considered ideal, to 30 meters desirable, and to at least 10 meters essential to achieving about 90% probability of survival. Note also that "clearing a defensible space" does not require an expanse of concrete or gravel; relatively non-flammable vegetation, such as a lawn or succulent, herbaceous plants and flowers, can provide comparable protection.[19]

The importance of landscapes in protecting structures can also be deduced from evidence from the 2002 Hayman fire, the largest wildfire in Colorado history. A total of 132 homes were burned in the Hayman fire. Of these, 70 (53%) "were destroyed in association with the occurrence of torching or crown fire in the home ignition zone. Sixty-two [47%] were destroyed by surface fire or firebrands."[20] Conversely, 662 homes—83% of the homes within the fire perimeter—survived the Hayman fire relatively unscathed.[21] Since 35% of the Hayman fire was a high-severity burn, and another 16% was a moderate-severity burn,[22] it seems likely that at least some of these homes (the number and portion are not documented) survived despite crown fire around them. Thus, it seems reasonable to conclude that the nature of the structure—rather the nature of the fire—primarily determines whether a structure survives a wildfire.

Responsibility for Protecting Structures

Owners are responsible for their structures. Insurance companies and the relevant state agencies that regulate insurance can contribute to structural protection by requiring certain materials and actions to obtain a policy for compensation following wildfire losses or by adjusting premiums based on homeowner actions. Local governmental agencies also play a role, since the building and zoning codes that could implement some of the safe-structure requirements are generally

---

(...continued)

[15] *Wildland/Urban Interface Fire Hazard Assessment Methodology*, p. 7.

[16] Jack D. Cohen, "Reducing the Wildland Fire Threat to Homes: Where and How Much?" *Proceedings of the Symposium on Fire Economics, Planning, and Policy: Bottom Lines*, Gen. Tech. Rept. PSW-GTR-173 (Berkeley, CA: USDA Forest Service, Pacific Southwest Research Station, Dec. 1999), pp. 189-195.

[17] Cohen, "Reducing the Wildland Fire Threat to Homes," p. 191.

[18] Cohen, "Reducing the Wildland Fire Threat to Homes," pp. 191-192.

[19] *FireSmart*, pp. 2-16.

[20] Jack Cohen and Rick Stratton, "Home Destruction Within the Hayman Fire Perimeter," *Hayman Fire Case Study*, Gen. Tech. Rept. RMRS-GTR-114 (Ft. Collins, CO: USDA Forest Service, Rocky Mountain Research Station, Sept. 2003): p. 264.

[21] Cohen and Stratton, "Home Destruction Within the Hayman Fire Perimeter," p. 263.

[22] Peter Robichaud, Lee MacDonald, Jeff Freeouf, Dan Neary, Deborah Martin, and Louise Ashman, "Postfire Rehabilitation of the Hayman Fire," *Hayman Fire Case Study*, Gen. Tech. Rept. RMRS-GTR-114 (Ft. Collins, CO: USDA Forest Service, Rocky Mountain Research Station, Sept. 2003), p. 294.

developed and enforced locally.[23] Alternatively, states can play a role; as of January 1, 2008, the California Building Standards Commission[24] is enforcing wildland-urban interface building standards in very high hazard zones.

The structure owners are also primarily responsible for the defensible space surrounding their structures. A 10-meter-wide clearing around a 3,000-square-foot structure encompasses less than a third of an acre—almost certainly private land owned in conjunction with the structure. Even a 40-meter clearing encompasses less than 2 acres, and thus is commonly part of the structure owner's property in the wildland-urban interface.

When a structural fire starts, the local fire department is responsible for controlling the blaze. State agencies may provide support for local fire departments, especially in the wildland-urban interface where a structural fire could cause a wildland fire. Occasionally, because of the location of firefighting resources, the federal agencies may be the first responders on a structural fire in the interface, but federal firefighters are generally not trained for safety in structural firefighting. The federal government has no responsibility for structural fire control in the wildland-urban interface. However, the Forest Service (FS) does have programs to provide technical and financial assistance to states and to volunteer fire departments.[25]

Given the nature of efforts needed to protect structures and the fact that developing, adopting, and enforcing building codes are local and state responsibilities, there is no clear federal responsibility in protecting structures from wildfires. However, the federal government often provides disaster assistance in the wake of a catastrophic wildfire, generally at the request of a governor. Federal disaster assistance is expensive and could be avoided if action to protect homes were taken in advance. Several federal agencies currently support FIREWISE, a program aimed at educating homeowners about how to make their structures safe from wildfire.[26] Assistance to homeowners—such as technical assistance, low-cost loans, and cost-sharing on projects—might be a cost-saving federal investment. Federal assistance to prepare local firefighters is another means for addressing home protection from wildfires.[27] Research on wildland-urban interface fire protection can also reduce losses.[28] Another possibility might be federal wildfire insurance,

---

[23] Model building codes for local governments exist. For example, in 2012, the International Code Council (ICC) published its International Wildland-Urban Interface Code (http://www.iccsafe.org/Store/Pages/Product.aspx?id= 3850X12#longdesc), with a separate chapter on ignition-resistant construction specifications. In June 2007, the National Fire Protection Association (NFPA) approved an updated standard, *Standard for Reducing Structure Ignition Hazards from Wildland Fire*, http://www.nfpa.org/aboutthecodes/AboutTheCodes.asp?DocNum=1144.

[24] See http://www.bsc.ca.gov/default.htm.

[25] For a description of these programs, see CRS Report RL31065, *Forestry Assistance Programs*, by Ross W. Gorte and Megan Stubbs.

[26] FIREWISE is part of the National Wildland/Urban Interface Fire Program, directed and sponsored by the Wildland/Urban Interface Working Team, which includes the USDA Forest Service, several DOI agencies (the Bureau of Land Management, Bureau of Indian Affairs, Fish and Wildlife Service, and National Park Service), and two agencies of the Department of Homeland Security (the Federal Emergency Management Agency and U.S. Fire Administration). It also includes the International Association of Fire Chiefs, National Association of State Fire Marshals, National Association of State Foresters, National Emergency Management Association, and National Fire Protection Association.

[27] See the program announced by the U.S. Fire Administration and the National Wildfire Coordinating Group, at https://www.usfa.dhs.gov/media/press/2008releases/012308.shtm.

[28] See the U.S. Forest Service Wildland-Urban Fire Models website, at http://www.fs.fed.us/pnw/fera/research/wfds/.

comparable to the National Flood Insurance Program.[29] Those living in an identified wildfire-prone zone would be required to purchase federal wildfire insurance (probably with an annual premium) to receive compensation for wildfire damages. The premiums could vary by eco-region, depending on the likelihood and risk of wildfires, and by aspects of the structure and landscaping (which might require periodic inspections).

Protecting Wildlands and Natural Resources

Wildlands and natural resources can also be damaged by wildfires. Wildfire damages vary widely, depending on the nature of the ecosystems burned as well as site-specific conditions. Activities to modify wildland biomass fuels can reduce damages, although the cost and effectiveness also vary. Finally, for fuel reduction activities on federal lands, delays and modifications—related to endangered species concerns and public involvement in decision-making—can affect the cost of fuel treatments.

Wildland Ecosystems and Wildfire

Ecosystem fire regimes can be classified in several ways; one common approach is to distinguish among surface fire ecosystems, stand-replacement fire ecosystems, and mixed fire ecosystems.[30] Damages to lands and resources depend on the nature of those ecosystems.

Surface Fire Ecosystems

Surface fire ecosystems are ecosystems where fires burn relatively frequently (typically 5- to 35-year intervals), with the fires consuming leaves or needles, grasses, twigs and small branches, and sometimes small trees, but generally leaving moderate and large trees unharmed by the fire. The classic surface fire ecosystem is the western Ponderosa pine, where seedlings occasionally survive the surface fire to become the scattered, stately pines in fields of grass or low brush. The other archetypical surface fire ecosystem is that of the southern yellow pines—shortleaf, slash, loblolly, and especially longleaf pine. Surface fire ecosystems account for about 34% of all U.S. wildlands.[31]

Over the past century, surface fire ecosystems in the West have been affected by grazing, logging, and fire protection. Heavy grazing reduced grass cover, which commonly carried the surface fires. Logging in many areas emphasized large pines, often leaving true firs and Douglas firs (which are more susceptible to drought, insect damage, and crown fires) to replace the pines, at least in the northern Rockies and Pacific Northwest. Fire protection has similarly led to more firs and Douglas firs, and small Ponderosa pines, than would typically have survived. With fire return

---

[29] For information on this program, see CRS Report RS22394, *National Flood Insurance Program: Treasury Borrowing in the Aftermath of Hurricane Katrina*, by Rawle O. King.

[30] Arno and Allison-Bunnell, *Flames in Our Forest*, pp. 44-45.

[31] Fire Modeling Institute, *Historical Fire Regimes by Current Condition Classes: Data Summary Tables* (Missoula, MT: USDA Forest Service, Rocky Mountain Research Station, Feb. 22, 2001), at http://www.fs.fed.us/fire/fuelman/data_summary_tables.pdf.

intervals of 5-35 years (i.e., fires typically burning once in that period), many surface fire ecosystems have missed two or more burning cycles. Thus, many forests now have an unnaturally large accumulation of small burnable materials and of trees susceptible to crown fires.

Many are concerned that the unnatural fuel accumulations and *fuel ladders* (continuous fuels from the ground to the tree crowns) from many small and medium-sized pines, firs, and Douglas firs are causing crown fires in ecosystems where such fires were rare. This could result in significant ecological damage to plants and animals ill-adapted to crown fires. It is unclear whether a new surface fire ecosystem will develop in the wake of an intense crown fire.

Research on fuel reduction treatments (discussed below) has documented the effectiveness of such treatments on Ponderosa pine (a surface fire ecosystem),[32] and activities that reduce fuel accumulations have been shown to reduce wildfire severity in surface fire ecosystems.[33] Presumably, less severe wildfires cause less damage to timber, to watersheds, and to wildlife and wildlife habitats.

Stand-Replacement Fire/Crown Fire Ecosystems

Stand-replacement fire ecosystems are those where crown fires are normal, natural, periodic events to which the ecosystem has adapted. The interval for the stand-replacement fires varies widely—from a few years (prairie grasses) to more than 1,000 years (coastal Douglas fir)—depending on the ecosystem. Some ecosystems require periodic crown fires to regenerate the ecosystem. For example, lodgepole pine in much of the West and jack pine in the Lake States have *serotinous* cones, which only open and release their seeds after exposure to temperatures exceeding 250° Fahrenheit. Similarly, chaparral in southern California and the desert Southwest, most perennial grasses, and aspen everywhere regenerate from rootstocks; burning the surface vegetation allows new plants to sprout from the underground stems, rhizomes, and root crowns. Stand-replacement fire ecosystems account for about 42% of all U.S. wildlands.[34]

It seems unlikely that stand-replacement fire ecosystems could suffer significant ecological damage from severe wildfires. In contrast to surface fire ecosystems, where crown fires could alter the ecosystem, in stand-replacement fire ecosystems, the *exclusion* of crown fires (if it were possible) would likely alter the ecosystems. This ecological change is implied by evidence from grass ecosystems (prairies and meadows), where fire suppression is feasible and which are being encroached upon by trees that would normally have been eliminated by the frequent fires.

Activities that reduce fuel levels in stand-replacement fire ecosystems have no documented effect on wildfire severity. Anecdotal reports have asserted that crown fires were halted (became surface fires) when they arrived at treated areas, but research has not documented where and when such

---

[32] Russell T. Graham, Alan E. Harvey, Theresa B. Jain, and Jonalea R. Tonn, *The Effects of Thinning and Similar Stand Treatments on Fire Behavior in Western Forests*, Gen. Tech. Rept. PNW-GTR-463 (Portland, OR: USDA Forest Service, Pacific Northwest Research Station, 1999).

[33] Philip N. Omi and Erik J. Martinson, *Final Report: Effect of Fuels Treatment on Wildfire Severity*, submitted to the Joint Fire Science Program Governing Board (Ft. Collins, CO: Colorado State Univ., Western Forest Fire Research Center, Mar. 25, 2002).

[34] *Historical Fire Regimes by Current Condition Classes*.

occurrences have happened. To date, no research has shown that fuel treatments consistently reduce the extent or severity of wildfires in stand-replacement fire ecosystems. The ineffectiveness of fuel reduction was particularly noted for southern California chaparral: "large fires were not dependent on old age classes of fuels, and it is thus unlikely that age class manipulation of fuels can prevent large fires."[35]

Mixed-Fire-Intensity Ecosystems

Many wildlands have ecosystems that burn in crown fires of relatively limited scale, substantially mixed with surface fires. These ecosystems are called mixed-fire-intensity ecosystems. A classic example is whitebark pine, a species generally limited to high elevation sites, near timberline (a demarcation where trees no longer grow). Whitebark pine is a slow-growing species that invades harsh sites and moderates the micro-climatic conditions to allow true firs and spruces to germinate and grow. The sporadic mixed-intensity fires kill most of the competing trees and some of the whitebark pines, but some pines survive. Also, burned sites are preferred "cache" sites for Clark's nutcrackers, which is the primary means of whitebark pine tree regeneration.[36] Other species that are commonly surface fire or stand-replacement fire species, such as Ponderosa pine and lodgepole pine, can be mixed-fire-intensity types under certain conditions, typically near the transition to another area with a different dominant tree species. Ponderosa pine, for example, may be a mixed-fire-intensity type on relatively moist sites, especially where it mixes naturally with Douglas fir, such as on north-facing slopes in the northern Rockies. Lodgepole pine may be a mixed-fire-intensity type on relatively dry sites, where the trees naturally grow farther apart, such as on the eastern slopes of the Sierra Nevada Mountains.

Less is known about wildfire in mixed-fire-intensity ecosystems, even though they occupy about 24% of U.S. wildlands.[37] It is unclear whether fuel loads have accumulated to unnatural levels, whether crown fires could cause significant ecological damage, or whether fuel reduction activities would alter wildfire extent or severity in these ecosystems.

Wildfire Effects

The effects of wildfires on natural resources are difficult to assess and are commonly overstated for two reasons. First, burned areas look bad—blackened trees and ground cover—even following surface fires. However, many plants recover from being burned. Conifers generally survive even with as much as 60% of their crowns scorched.[38] Other plants, especially grasses, aspen, and some brush species, resprout vigorously after being burned. Furthermore, animals (regardless of their size and mobility) are rarely killed by wildfire.[39]

---

[35] Jon E. Keeley, C. J. Fotheringham, and Marco Marais, "Reexamining Fire Suppression Impacts on Brushland Fire Regimes," *Science*, v. 284 (June 11, 1999), p. 1829.

[36] Diana F. Tomback, "Clark's Nutcracker; Agent of Regeneration," *Whitebark Pine Ecology and Restoration*, Diana F. Tomback, Stephen F. Arno, and Robert E. Keane, eds. (Washington, DC, Island Press, 2001), pp. 90-100.

[37] *Historical Fire Regimes by Current Condition Classes*.

[38] See Ross W. Gorte, *Fire Effects Appraisal: The Wisconsin DNR Example*, Ph.D. dissertation (East Lansing, MI: Michigan State Univ., June 1981).

[39] L. Jack Lyon, Mark H. Huff, Robert G. Hooper, Edmund S. Telfer, David Scott Schreiner, and Jane Kapler Smith, (continued...)

The other reason that wildfire effects are commonly overstated is that the reported burned area includes all the acres within the fire perimeter. However, even severe crown fires are patchy, leaving some areas lightly burned or unburned. For example, in the Yellowstone fires that were on the nightly news for weeks in the summer of 1988, 30% of the reported burned area was actually unburned and another 15%-20% had only surface fire.[40] In the 2002 Hayman fire, the worst wildfire in Colorado history, 35% of the area had a high-severity burn and 16% had a moderate-severity burn; 34% had a low-severity burn and 15% was unburned.[41] Thus, severely burned acreage is substantially less than the burned area that is reported.

Severe wildfires can cause long-lasting resource damages. Crown fires kill many plants within the burned area, increasing the potential for erosion until the vegetation recovers. Some observers have reported "soil glassification," where the silica in the soils has been melted and fused, forming an impermeable layer in the soil, although research has yet to document the extent, frequency, and duration of the condition and the soils and conditions in which it occurs. Landslides can also occur in areas with unstable soils where the vegetation has burned, such as in coastal southern California. Timber can also be damaged, although burned trees can often be salvaged for lumber and other wood products. However, harvesting and processing costs are typically higher in burned areas, and many object to post-fire salvage harvesting because of its possible additional impacts on soils and other resource values. Wildfires, especially crown fires, can also have significant local economic effects—directly on tourism, and indirectly through effects on timber supply, water quality, and aesthetics. On the other hand, federal wildfire suppression efforts include substantial expenditures, many of which are made locally, and fire-fighting jobs are considered financially desirable in many areas.[42]

Protecting Wildlands and Resources

The federal government is generally responsible for protecting federal lands and their natural resources from wildfire.[43] Wildfire protection of other wildlands and natural resources—state, local government, and private lands—is the responsibility of the states, although the individual landowners are responsible for excessive fuel accumulations and other hazardous conditions on their own lands. As noted above, the FS has a technical and financial assistance program for state fire agencies.

The principal goal for land and resource protection is to reduce the damages caused by wildfires. This can best be achieved by reducing burnable biomass (live and dead) to reduce wildfire intensity and duration, and especially by eliminating the *fuel ladders* (relatively continuous

---

(...continued)

Wildland Fire in Ecosystems: Effects of Fire on Fauna, Gen. Tech. Rept. RMRS-GTR-42-vol. 1 (Ogden, UT: USDA Forest Service, Rocky Mountain Research Station, Jan. 2000).

[40] Lyon, et al., *Effects of Fire on Fauna*, p. 44.

[41] Robichaud et al., "Postfire Rehabilitation of the Hayman Fire," p. 294.

[42] Nelson, *A Burning Issue*, pp. 37-38.

[43] The federal government also protects some state and private lands where the landowner has a cooperative agreement with a federal agency, while some federal lands similarly are protected by state or private organizations under cooperative agreements.

---

biomass from the surface to tree crowns) that facilitate wildfire transition from a surface fire to a crown fire.[44] Fuel treatments can also reduce the *crown bulk density* (the biomass, especially fine fuels, in the tree crowns), making it more difficult for a crown fire to sustain itself, thus making a wildfire more controllable.[45] Reducing burnable biomass, however, does not eliminate wildfires, because fuel reduction does not directly alter the dryness of the biomass or the probability of an ignition.

The two principal mechanisms for reducing fuels are prescribed burning and mechanical treatments, although the two tools can also be combined. Each tool has benefits, costs, and risks or limitations to its use.

Prescribed Burning

Prescribed burning is intentionally setting fires in specified areas when fuel and weather conditions are within prescribed limits (e.g., fuel moisture content, relative humidity, wind speed). Some observers include, in their definition of prescribed burning, naturally occurring fires that are allowed to burn because they are within acceptable areas and conditions, as identified in fire management plans. The agencies term such fires *wildland fire use*, and do not identify them as prescribed fires, but do include the acres burned in wildland-fire-use fires as acres treated for fuel reduction.

Prescribed burning is used for reducing biomass fuels because it is the only means available for eliminating *fine fuels* (grasses, needles, leaves, forbs, and twigs and shrubs less than a quarter-inch in diameter [pencil-sized]). Burning converts the vegetation to smoke (carbon dioxide, water vapor, fine particulates, and other pollutants) and ashes (mineralized forms of the organic matter, readily available for absorption by new plant growth). Reducing fine fuels is critical in wildfire protection and control, because fine fuels are necessary to carry wildfires; without fine fuels, wildfires cannot spread.

Prescribed burning has various limitations. Smoke can be a problem, contributing to human health problems, especially in areas where inversions are common or with relatively stagnant airsheds. Also, prescribed burning is risky. It is not *controlled* burning; there is no such thing as controlled burning, because there is no switch to turn the fire off. Prescribed fire is also an indiscriminate tool for reducing tree density, crown density, and fuel ladders, burning what is available, depending on a host of site-specific and micro-climatic conditions.

Finally, prescribed burning is expensive. Actually starting the prescribed fire is cheap—matches don't cost a lot. However, minimizing the risk to surrounding areas (especially private lands and housing developments) requires planning and preparation as well as sufficient trained personnel and supervisors to react when unexpected fire behavior occurs or weather conditions change. Prescribed burning costs are estimated to range from $12 to $174 per acre, depending on the fuel type, treatment method, size of area to be treated, steepness of slopes, site elevation, and other

---

[44] Russell T. Graham, Alan E. Harvey, Theresa B. Jain, and Jonalea R. Tonn, *The Effects of Thinning and Similar Stand Treatments on Fire Behavior in Western Forests*, Gen. Tech. Rept. PNW-GTR-463 (Portland, OR: USDA Forest Service, Pacific Northwest Research Station, 1999).

[45] Graham et al., *The Effects of Thinning on Fire Behavior*.

factors.[46] A prescribed fire that becomes a wildfire, such as the Cerro Grande fire in Los Alamos, NM (which burned 239 houses in town), raises questions about the practice and about the fire managers who use it. Thus, fire managers tend to err on the side of excessive personnel (and cost) for a prescribed fire, rather than risk a costly, damaging wildfire with far higher costs.

Mechanical Treatment

Mechanical fuel treatment includes a wide array of activities designed to reduce biomass on a site. Foresters have a variety of terms for the various activities, including:[47]

- pruning—removing lower tree branches, which eliminates fuel ladders and can reduce crown density.

- release—removing several to many trees from a young stand (saplings or smaller) to concentrate wood growth on desirable trees, which reduces crown density.

- thinning—removing a portion of the standing trees; the portion can vary widely from very light (relatively few trees) to very heavy (more than half the trees in the stand). Thinning can be commercial (if the trees are large enough for products) or precommercial. It can be used to eliminate fuel ladders and reduce crown density, depending on the approach and portion of trees removed. Thinning approaches include:

  —low thinning, or thinning from below, to remove the smallest and poorest specimens, which eliminates fuel ladders and can reduce crown density;

  —crown thinning, or thinning from above, to open the canopy to stimulate growth on the remaining trees, which substantially reduces crown density;

  —selection thinning, to remove the least desirable trees for the future stand, which reduces crown density and can eliminate fuel ladders; and

  —mechanical thinning, to provide appropriate spacing for the remaining trees, which reduces crown density and can eliminate fuel ladders.

- salvage harvesting—removing a portion to all of the standing trees, many of which have been killed or are in imminent danger. This includes presalvage harvesting (removing highly vulnerable trees before they are killed) and sanitation harvesting (removing trees to control the spread of insects or diseases). It reduces (or eliminates) crown bulk density, and might reduce fuel ladders.

---

[46] U.S. Forest Service, *Fuels Planning: Science Synthesis and Integration—Economic Uses Fact Sheet: 8—Prescribed Fire Costs*, December 2004, http://www.fs.fed.us/rm/pubs/rmrs_rn020_08.pdf.

[47] For more information, see David M. Smith, Bruce C. Larson, Matthew J. Kelty, and Mark S. Ashton, *The Practice of Silviculture: Applied Forest Ecology*, 9th ed. (New York, NY: John Wiley & Sons, 1997).

Treatment Choices

Mechanical fuel treatment clearly involves choices—about the amount of biomass to be removed, and about the nature of the biomass to be removed (small and weak trees, lower limbs, vulnerable trees or species, etc.). The choice can also be over the method used for the treatment: a commercial sale, if the treatment yields commercially usable wood; a stewardship contract, if commercially usable wood can be exchanged for other activities; a service contract, for specified actions; an end-results contract, to specify what is left after treatment; or even treatment by agency personnel. All of these choices affect public acceptance of the proposed treatment.

Benefits and Limitations

The primary benefit of mechanical fuel treatment is the high degree of control over the results. One report stated:[48]

> Mechanical thinning has the ability to more precisely create targeted stand structure than does prescribed fire.... Used alone, mechanical thinning, especially emphasizing the smaller trees and shrubs, can be effective in reducing the vertical fuel continuity that fosters initiation of crown fires. In addition, thinning of small material and pruning branches are more precise methods than prescribed fire for targeting ladder fuels and specific fuel components.

The authors also observed some of the limitations of mechanical fuel treatment:[49]

> However, by itself mechanical thinning does little to beneficially affect surface fuels with the exception of possibly compacting, crushing, or masticating it during the thinning process. Depending on how it is accomplished, mechanical thinning may add to surface fuels (and increase surface fire intensity) unless the fine fuels that result from the thinning are removed from the stand or otherwise treated....

> Thinning and prescribed fires can modify understory microclimate that was previously buffered by overstory vegetation.... Thinned stands (open tree canopies) allow solar radiation to penetrate to the forest floor, which then increases surface temperatures, decreases fire fuel moisture, and decreases relative humidity compared to unthinned stands—conditions that can increase surface fire intensity.... An increase in surface fire intensity may increase the likelihood that overstory tree crowns ignite.

Other sources have similarly reported the limitations of thinning:[50]

> Depending on the forest type and its structure, thinning has both positive and negative impacts on crown fire potential. Crown bulk density, surface fuel , and crown base height [fuel ladders] are primary stand characteristics that determine crown fire potential. Thinning from below, free thinning, and reserve tree shelterwoods have the greatest opportunity for reducing the risk of crown fire behavior. Selection thinning and crown thinning that maintain multiple crown layers ...

---

[48] Russell T. Graham, Sarah McCaffery, and Theresa N. Jain, tech. eds., *Science Basis for Changing Forest Structure to Modify Wildfire Behavior and Severity*, Gen. Tech. Rept. RMRS-GTR-120 (Ft. Collins, CO: USDA Forest Service, Rocky Mountain Research Station, Apr. 2004), p. 25.

[49] Graham, et al., *Science Basis for Changing Forest Structure*, pp. 25, 27.

[50] Graham, et al., *The Effects of Thinning on Fire Behavior*, abstract.

will not reduce the risk of crown fires except in the driest ponderosa pine ... forests. Moreover, unless the surface fuels created by using these treatments are themselves treated, intense surface wildfire may result, likely negating positive effects of reducing crown fire potential. No single thinning approach can be applied to reduce the risk of wildfires in the multiple forest types of the West.

Thus, thinning and pruning have the potential to reduce the risk of crown fire, but may *increase* wildfire risk until the *slash* (non-commercial biomass) degrades (rots or burns, typically in a few years to decades, depending on the ecosystem), or is removed. In addition, thinning is an expensive proposition, with treatment costs ranging "from $35 to over $1000 per acre depending on the type of operation, terrain, and number of trees to be treated."[51]

Commercial operations—commercial thinning, stewardship contracting, and salvage logging—have been suggested as a means to moderate the high cost of mechanical fuel treatment. However, commercial timber sales on federal lands commonly cost more to prepare and administer than they return to the Treasury.[52] The results of commercial operations for fuel reduction are also questionable:[53]

> The proposal that **commercial logging** can reduce the incidence of canopy fires was untested in the scientific literature. Commercial logging focuses on large diameter trees and does not address crown base height—the branches, seedlings and saplings which contribute so significantly to the "ladder effect" in wildfire behavior.

Others have also noted the likely net cost of thinning to reduce the risk of crown fires:[54]

> Although large trees can be removed for valuable products, the market value for the smaller logs may be less than the harvest and hauling charges, resulting in a net cost for thinning operations. However, the failure to remove these small logs results in the retention of ladder fuels that support crown fires with destructive impacts to the forest landscape. A cost/benefit analysis broadened to include market and nonmarket considerations indicates that the negative impacts of crown fires are underestimated and that the benefits of government investments in fuel reductions are substantial.

Combined Operations

The ability to control the resulting stand structure with mechanical treatments and the ability to remove fine fuels with prescribed burning make combining the two treatments seem a logical

---

[51] *A Strategic Assessment of Forest Biomass and Fuel Reduction Treatment in Western States*, Gen. Tech. Rept. RMRS-GTR-149 (Ft. Collins, CO: USDA Forest Service, Rocky Mountain Research Station, 2005).

[52] CRS Report RL32485, *Below-Cost Timber Sales: An Overview*, by Ross W. Gorte.

[53] Henry Carey and Martha Schumann, *Modifying WildFire Behavior—The Effectiveness of Fuel Treatments: The Status of Our Knowledge*, Southwest Region Working Paper 2 (Santa Fe, NM: National Community Forestry Center, April 2003), pp. i-ii.

[54] C. Larry Mason, Bruce R. Lippke, Kevin W. Zobrist, Thomas D. Bloxton, Jr., Kevin R. Cedar, Jeffrey M. Comnick, James B. McCarter, and Heather K. Rogers, "Investments in Fuel Removal to Avoid Forest Fires Result in Substantial Benefits," *Journal of Forestry*, v. 104 (Jan./Feb. 2006): p. 27.

choice. However, empirical evidence to document the effectiveness of such combined operations is limited:[55]

> A more limited number of studies addressed the effectiveness of a **combination of thinning and burning** in moderating wildfire behavior. The impacts varied, depending on the treatment of the thinning slash prior to burning.

In addition, the cost of combined operations is substantially greater than the cost of either alone.

Area Needing Treatment

The areas that might benefit from prescribed burning and/or mechanical treatment are not entirely clear. **Table 1**, below, shows the acreage of national forest land, Department of the Interior land, and all other land by (a) historical fire regime (comparable to the ecosystem types described above); and (b) condition class—low risk (Class 1), moderate risk (Class 2), and high risk (Class 3) of losing key ecosystem components in a wildfire.

Based on the discussion above of the effectiveness of various treatments, it seems reasonable to conclude that treating lands in the Class 3 (high risk), low severity (surface fire) regime could reduce the likelihood of crown fires in these ecosystems, where such fires are unnatural (or at least very rare). **Table 1** shows this to include 28.8 million acres of national forest land, 6.5 million acres of Interior land, and 42.2 million acres of other federal, state, and private land.

Table 1. Lands at Risk of Ecological Damage from Wildfire, by Landowner Group and Historical Fire Regime

(in millions of acres)

Landowner/Historical Fire Regime	Total	Class 1 (low risk)	Class 2 (mod. risk)	Class 3 (high risk)
USDA Forest Service				
Low severity (surface fire)	83.67	19.87	34.96	28.83
Mixed severity	53.93	16.05	26.71	11.17
Stand replacement	58.93	29.03	18.77	11.13
Forest Service, total	**196.52**	**64.95**	**80.45**	**51.12**
Dept. of the Interior				
Low severity (surface fire)	49.00	18.70	23.83	6.46
Mixed severity	97.80	62.05	25.82	9.92
Stand replacement	80.93	47.67	26.17	7.09
Interior Dept., total	**227.72**	**128.42**	**75.83**	**23.47**
Other federal, state, and private lands				
Low severity (surface fire)	296.02	136.46	117.37	42.20

[55] Carey and Schumann, *Modifying WildFire Behavior*, pp. i-ii.

Landowner/Historical Fire Regime	Total	Class 1 (low risk)	Class 2 (mod. risk)	Class 3 (high risk)
Mixed severity	142.18	49.55	59.72	32.92
Stand replacement	386.81	217.46	137.28	32.07
Other lands, total	**825.01**	**404.60**	**313.24**	**107.18**

Source: Kirsten M. Schmidt, James P. Menakis, Colin C. Hardy, Wendel J. Hann, and David L. Bunnell, *Development of Coarse-Scale Spatial Data for Wildland Fire and Fuel Management*, Gen. Tech. Rept. RMRS-87 (Ft. Collins, CO: USDA Forest Service, Rocky Mountain Research Station, Apr. 2002), pp. 13-15.

The cost to treat these lands varies widely. One study, cited above, reported mechanical treatment costs of $35 to $1,000 per acre, depending on terrain, type of operation, and number of trees to be cut.[56] Others have similarly reported highly variable costs for commercial mechanical treatment above and below the "base case" cost of $150 per acre, depending on tree size, stand density, terrain, and whether the treatment was conducted in the wildland-urban interface.[57] The same source reported similar variability in costs for prescribed burning, above and below the "base case" cost of $105 per acre. Federal appropriations for fuel treatment averaged about $170 per acre for FY2001-FY2006—$165 per acre for the Forest Service and $174 per acre for the BLM.[58] The General Accounting Office (GAO, now the Government Accountability Office) used a Forest Service estimate of $300 per acre in its 1999 estimate of needed funding for fuel treatment, because of the higher cost per acre to treat additional western lands.[59] At $300 per acre, Forest Service costs to treat the Class 3 surface fire regime lands would be $8.6 billion, and Department of the Interior costs would be $1.9 billion. Other surface (low severity) fire regime lands might also warrant treatment, although the lower risk of ecological damage suggests a lower priority for treatment.

It is unclear whether any lands other than the surface fire regime lands warrant fuel treatment. The existing research evidence on fuel treatment for stand-replacement fire regimes raises questions about the effectiveness of both mechanical treatment and prescribed fire for reducing the likelihood of damages from a crown fire. One might even question whether ecological damage can be ascribed to a crown fire in a stand-replacement fire ecosystem, since these ecosystems have evolved adaptations to reestablish themselves following crown fires. Evidence is also lacking about the effectiveness of mechanical treatments and prescribed burning on mixed-intensity fire ecosystems. Thus, it is not certain whether fuel treatment on these mixed-intensity fire regime lands and stand-replacement fire regime lands would provide any significant wildfire protection.

---

[56] *A Strategic Assessment of Forest Biomass.*

[57] Roger D. Fight and R. James Barbour, *Financial Analysis of Fuel Treatments*, Gen. Tech. Rept. PNW-GTR-662 (Portland, OR: USDA Forest Service, Pacific Northwest Research Station, Dec. 2005).

[58] Data from annual agency budget justifications, presented in CRS Report RL33990, *Federal Funding for Wildfire Control and Management*, by Ross W. Gorte and Kelsi Bracmort.

[59] GAO, *Western National Forests: A Cohesive Strategy Is Needed to Address Catastrophic Wildfire Threats*, GAO/RCED-99-65 (Washington, DC: April 1999). The Forest Service has done more fuel treatment in the South, where the generally gentler terrains, denser and more uniform timber stands, and historic fire patterns have kept treatment costs per acre lower than in the West.

Delays and Changes in Federal Decision-Making

Some advocates of fuel treatment are concerned that delays and changes to the implementation of fuel treatments might lead to catastrophic crown fires that could have been prevented by more expeditious fuel treatment. Concerns are generally linked to consultations under the Endangered Species Act (ESA, P.L. 93-205; 16 U.S.C. §§1531-1544), and to public involvement under the National Environmental Policy Act of 1969 (NEPA; P.L. 91-190, 42 U.S.C. §§4321-4347) and the Forest Service Appeals Reform Act (ARA; §322 of P.L. 102-381, the FY1993 Interior Appropriations Act, 16 U.S.C. §1612 note).[60]

Involving the public and consulting over possible impacts on endangered or threatened species take time, and concerns and objections can delay, modify, or even prevent some proposed actions. However, others caution that expedited review or limits on ESA consultation and on public oversight of proposed fuel treatments may allow treatments to include commercial timber harvests or other actions that provide little wildfire protection and exacerbate fuel accumulations in the short run, while causing other environmental damages.

This raises the question of the effect of delays on wildfire threats. Clearly, structures in the wildland-urban interface are threatened by wildfire, but as shown above, fuel treatment provides little, if any, fire protection for structures, and thus delaying fuel treatments has little consequence for structure protection. Resources in surface fire ecosystems with unnatural fuel accumulations are at risk from severe wildfires. The odds of having treated the "right" acres to prevent a crown fire with significant resource damages are, however, quite low. For the past decade, during which more area burned than in any other decade since 1960, wildfires have burned an average of 7.0 million acres annually. Total wildlands in the United States are 1.45 *billion* acres—roughly 640 million acres of federal land,[61] and roughly 815 million acres of private forest and rangeland.[62] Thus, the likelihood of any particular acre burning in any given year, on average, is less than 0.66% (i.e., burning once every 150 years). Obviously, the risk for certain areas in particular years can be much higher—5.4% of Idaho's wildlands burned in 2007, for example—but this is offset by much lower risks for those areas in other years and for other areas in the same year—0.2% of Idaho's wildlands burned in 2002, while 0.04% of Colorado wildlands burned in 2007, in contrast to 1.8% in 2002, when the Hayman fire burned.[63] Wildfire risk is probably somewhat higher in western states than the national average, because the ecosystems in the Lake States, mid-Atlantic region, and New England experience less fire; however, even if the risk were 50% greater than the national average (which seems unlikely because the larger area in the West already contributes to a higher national average), the risk would still be less than 1% per year.

In addition to the low probability of a particular acre burning is the modest likelihood of an area being treated. The Forest Service and BLM treated 2.7 million acres of their lands annually from

---

[60] See CRS Report RL32436, *Public Participation in the Management of Forest Service and Bureau of Land Management Lands: Overview and Recent Changes*, by Pamela Baldwin.

[61] See CRS Report R42346, *Federal Land Ownership: Overview and Data*, by Ross W. Gorte et al.

[62] Includes acres of private forests and rangelands in the coterminous 48 states. U.S. Dept. of Agriculture, Natural Resources Conservation Service, *Summary Report 2007 National Resources Inventory*, December 2009, p. 6.

[63] See CRS memoranda on *Wildfire and Wildland Data*, by Ross W. Gorte, June 20, 2003, and March 3, 2008, available from the author.

FY2003 through FY2007.[64] This is less than 8% of their Class 3 surface fire ecosystem lands, and less than 3% of Class 3 plus Class 2 surface fire ecosystem lands. If the same acreage of treatments are spread more broadly—to Class 1 surface fire ecosystem lands or to lands in other fire regimes—the probability of treating a particular acre to prevent a crown fire diminishes further.

Nonetheless, lengthy delays can exacerbate the risks. Annual probabilities of a wildfire burning an area and of an area being treated are both cumulative. Over a 10-year period, the likelihood of an area burning is more than 6%, while the likelihood of a moderate- or high-risk surface fire ecosystem being treated rises to 15% (if half of all treatments are concentrated on these lands). Thus, relatively brief delays may have relatively little impact of the likelihood of an area being burned in an unnatural crown fire, but longer delays (a decade or more) could have a significant impact.

ESA Consultations[65]

The ESA established a process for federal agencies to consult with the Fish and Wildlife Service (FWS), or with the National Marine Fisheries Service (NMFS) for some species, on any actions that *might* jeopardize a listed endangered or threatened species or adversely modify its critical habitat. This is not a problem for firefighting, as immediate, informal consultations can occur during an emergency, with formal consultation to follow after the emergency has passed. However, some fuel treatments might jeopardize a species or adversely modify its habitat, which would require ESA consultation. Consultation means the FWS (or NMFS) would review the proposed action and, if jeopardy or adverse habitat impacts are likely, propose a "reasonable and prudent alternative" to achieve the same purpose without jeopardy or adverse habitat modification. The vast majority of agency activities have a finding of no jeopardy, and most with jeopardy have a reasonable and prudent alternative; actions with jeopardy and no alternative findings are exceedingly rare.

Fuel treatments that reduce the likelihood of crown fires in ecosystems where such fires were historically rare are generally unlikely to jeopardize or adversely modify the critical habitat of endangered species. Many species in North America are adapted to survive and even thrive with natural wildfires. One study reported that more than 90% of rare, threatened, and endangered plants in the 48 coterminous states either benefit from fire or are found in fire-adapted ecosystems.[66] Also, as noted above, animal mortality in wildfires is rare. Thus, treatments that only restore forests to conditions that allow a historically natural ecological role for wildfire are more likely to benefit endangered and threatened species than to harm them.

---

[64] See Table 6 in CRS Report RL33990, *Federal Funding for Wildfire Control and Management*, by Ross W. Gorte and Kelsi Bracmort. The agencies no longer report fuel treatment on the same basis, and thus actual treatments since FY2007 are not analyzed.

[65] For information on ESA generally, see CRS Report RL31654, *The Endangered Species Act: A Primer*, by M. Lynne Corn, Kristina Alexander, and Eugene H. Buck.

[66] Amy Hessl and Susan Spackman, *Effects of Fire on Threatened and Endangered Plants: An Annotated Bibliography*, Information and Technical Report 2 (Ft. Collins, CO: U.S. Dept. of the Interior, National Biological Service, n.d.).

Nonetheless, ESA consultations take time, and can delay fuel treatments. This is more likely to be the case when restoration treatments (e.g., prescribed burning or thinning from below) are combined with other activities (e.g., commercial timber harvesting), such as in a stewardship contract. Thus, the method used to undertake the treatment, as well as the nature of the treatment itself, determines the length of delays and possible project modifications from ESA consultations.

NEPA Environmental Analysis and Public Involvement[67]

NEPA requires federal agencies to review the environmental effects of "major Federal actions significantly affecting the quality of the human environment." Agencies must consider every significant aspect of the environmental impacts of a proposed action before making an irreversible commitment of resources to the project. NEPA also requires that agencies inform the public that they have considered those impacts in their decision-making process. In his executive order on NEPA implementation, President Richard Nixon directed the agencies to go beyond just informing the public, to actively involve the public early in the decision-making process.[68] Fuel reduction treatments to protect resources from wildfires are generally considered to be major federal actions subject to NEPA.

Environmental Analysis

The action agency must analyze the possible environmental consequences of its actions. The first step is to determine if the action will have significant environmental impacts. There are three possible outcomes. If significant impacts are likely, then the agency prepares an environmental impact statement (EIS). If the impacts are normally insignificant—individually and cumulatively—the activity can be *categorically excluded* from further NEPA environmental analysis and public involvement. (See below.) If the significance of the impacts is uncertain, the agency prepares an environmental assessment (EA) to determine the significance of the impacts. The EA leads either to a finding of no significant impact (FONSI) or to an EIS.

Advocates of expedited fuel treatment are concerned about the time needed to prepare an EIS or even an EA. Information collection and analysis may take from several days to a few months, depending on the magnitude and complexity of the proposed action. An EIS involves additional steps to assess the likely and the possible environmental impacts and to inform and involve the public. These steps include *scoping* (public discussions about the nature, location, and possible consequences of the proposal); a draft EIS, examining a range of alternatives and generally identifying a preferred alternative; public comments on the draft and the preferred alternative; and then a final EIS and record of decision (ROD).[69] Only after completing this process—which can take a year or more for large, complex projects—can the agency undertake the action. Thus,

---

[67] For more information on NEPA generally, see CRS Report RL33152, *The National Environmental Policy Act (NEPA): Background and Implementation*, by Linda Luther, and CRS Report RS20621, *Overview of National Environmental Policy Act (NEPA) Requirements*, by Kristina Alexander.

[68] Executive Order 11514, "Protection and Enhancement of Environmental Quality," 35 *Fed. Reg.* 4247 (March 5, 1970).

[69] A simplified flowchart of this process can be found in CRS Report RL33152, *The National Environmental Policy Act (NEPA): Background and Implementation*, by Linda Luther.

---

proponents of expeditious fuel reduction projects often advocate various approaches to accelerate the process, discussed below.

Categorical Exclusions (CEs)

As noted above, certain projects can be categorically excluded from the requirement to prepare an EA or an EIS. Such a CE action is defined as:[70]

> a category of actions which do not individually or cumulatively have a significant effect on the human environment ... and for which, therefore, neither an environmental assessment nor an environmental impact statement is required.... Any procedures under this section shall provide for extraordinary circumstances in which a normally excluded action may have a significant environmental effect.

CEs are typically used for relatively minor, routine actions (e.g., thinning, debris removal) that the agency does frequently and has found to have at most insignificant environmental impacts. For projects approved under CEs, the Forest Service is not required to provide notice and opportunity for public comment as otherwise required for agency activities under the ARA. (See below.)

In certain situations—such as those involving controversial issues (e.g., wetlands and roadless areas) or specifically protected resources (e.g., endangered species and archaeological sites)—known as *extraordinary circumstances*, CEs cannot be used. In 2002, the Forest Service modified its application of extraordinary circumstances, allowing the responsible official to determine whether the extraordinary circumstances warranted an EA or an EIS, rather than automatically precluding use of a CE in the presence of extraordinary circumstances.[71]

The Forest Service has identified numerous categories of actions for which a CE may be used; two relate directly to wildfire protection (for details on Forest Service CEs and extraordinary circumstances, see the **Appendix**):[72]

> 6. *Timber stand and/or wildlife habitat improvement activities* ..., [including] thinning or brush control to improve growth or reduce fire hazard ..., prescribed burning to control understory hardwoods in stands of southern pine, [and] prescribed burning to reduce natural fuel build-up....

> 10. *Hazardous fuel reduction activities using prescribed fire, not to exceed 4,500 acres, and mechanical methods for crushing, piling, thinning, pruning, cutting, chipping, mulching, and mowing, not to exceed 1,000 acres* ... limited to ... the wildland-urban interface; or Condition Classes 2 or 3 [moderate or high risk of ecological damage] in Fire Regimes I, II, or III [surface fire, stand-replacement fire with a return interval of 35 years or less, and mixed-intensity fire]. (emphasis in original)

---

[70] 40 C.F.R. §1508.4.

[71] 67 *Fed. Reg.* 54622 (Aug. 23, 2002).

[72] Forest Service Handbook, National Headquarters (WO), Washington, DC, *FSH 1909.15—Environmental Policy and Procedures Handbook. Chapter 30—Categorical Exclusion from Documentation*, Amendment No. 1909.15-2007-1 (Feb. 15, 2007).

Forest Service use of the latter CE was halted after a court found it was arbitrary and capricious.[73] Other CEs have also been challenged, raising questions about the availability of CEs for fuel reduction projects.[74]

Forest Service Appeals Reform Act

In addition to public involvement under NEPA, the Forest Service must also inform the public of its decisions and provide an opportunity for the public to request an administrative review of its decisions under the Forest Service Decisionmaking and Appeals Reform Act (ARA).[75] Subsections (a) and (b) require the Forest Service to provide notice and an opportunity for public comment on proposed actions; this is the only provision requiring notice and comment on Forest Service proposals other than under NEPA. Subsections (c) and (d) specify an administrative appeals process—review by a higher-ranking official—for those who had commented on the proposal and object to the decision.

GAO was asked to examine administrative appeals of fuel reduction projects.[76] For FY2001 and FY2002, prior to promulgation of the hazardous fuel reduction CE, 59% of fuel reduction projects used CEs and could not be appealed. Of those that could be appealed, 58% were appealed (i.e., 24% of all fuel reduction projects during that period). Of those, 73% were implemented without change, 8% were modified, and 19% (less than 5% of all projects) were withdrawn or reversed. Furthermore, 79% of the appeals were resolved within the prescribed 90 days. These data are supported by a study of all Forest Service administrative appeals.[77] This study found that 8% of appeals were granted (i.e., decision reversed) and that 9% of appealed decisions were withdrawn.

A different study examined factors that increased the likelihood of a fuel reduction project being appealed.[78] It reported that appeals were more likely for fuel reduction projects that (1) affected more area; (2) included more activities for the site; (3) included commercial timber harvest; (4) included as a purpose reducing fuels generated by the project; and (5) had at least one threatened or endangered mammal near the site. These factors are indirectly confirmed in the GAO study, since 92% of projects with EISs (larger projects with likely environmental impacts) were appealed, compared to 52% of projects with EAs (projects with uncertain environmental impacts).[79] Conversely, projects were significantly less likely to be appealed if the project was (1)

---

[73] *Sierra Club v. Bosworth*, 510 F. 3d 1016 (9th Cir. 2007).

[74] For information on the status of relevant judicial decisions, see CRS Report R40237, *Federal Lands Managed by the Bureau of Land Management (BLM) and the Forest Service (FS): Issues in the 111th Congress*, coordinated by Ross W. Gorte and Carol Hardy Vincent.

[75] Section 322 of the Department of the Interior and Related Agencies Appropriations Act, 1993 (P.L. 102-381; 16 U.S.C. §1612 note). The appeals process under the ARA, including the public notice and comment period, will change to a pre-decisional objection process as soon as final regulations are issued (P.L. 112-74 §428). The law does not establish a time frame for issuing the regulations.

[76] GAO, *Forest Service: Information on Appeals and Litigation Involving Fuels Reduction Activities*, GAO-04-52 (Washington, DC, Oct. 2003).

[77] Gretchen M. R. Teich, Jacqueline Vaughn, and Hanna J. Cortner, "National Trends in the Use of Forest Service Administrative Appeals," *Journal of Forestry*, vol. 102 (March 2004): pp. 14-19.

[78] David N. LaBand, Armando González-Cabán, and Anwar Hussain, "Factors That Influence Administrative Appeals of Proposed USDA Forest Service Fuels Reduction Actions," *Forest Science*, vol. 52, no. 2 (2006): pp. 477-488.

[79] GAO, *Information on Appeals of Fuel Reduction Activities*.

---

implemented by Forest Service personnel or a service contract; and (2) in the wildland-urban interface.

These data suggest that administrative appeals are less of a problem than the advocates of fuel treatment suggest. Only about a quarter of proposed projects are appealed, with less than 5% prevented from being implemented, and delays of less than 90 days for most projects. However, for prescribed burning, a 90-day delay can be significant, since the period within the prescribed conditions can be brief.

Expedited Procedures

Proponents of aggressive fuel treatment continue to be concerned about delays from the ESA, NEPA, and ARA review processes, and have pressed for various means for accelerating the reviews. Some procedures are currently feasible under existing regulations, others have been enacted by Congress in various contexts, and more have been proposed.

Expedited ESA Consultations

As noted above, during emergencies, the agencies can consult informally for rapid action, with formal consultations to follow when the situation has stabilized. This clearly applied during wildfire suppression activities, but fuel reduction treatments are not emergency actions that require an immediate response to prevent damages. As discussed above, lengthy (multi-year) delays in fuel reduction activities can increase the likelihood of resource damages from wildfires, but brief delays have minor impacts.

The agencies have developed an alternative approach to ESA consultations that is intended to accelerate the ESA review process: *counterpart* regulations.[80] These regulations allow the Forest Service, BLM, and others to assess whether the proposed fuel reduction action is likely to jeopardize a listed threatened or endangered species or to adversely modify critical habitat, rather than to consult with the Fish and Wildfire Service on the likelihood of jeopardy or adverse habitat modification. While some ESA counterpart regulations have been challenged successfully, the counterpart regulations related to wildfire management remain in place.[81]

Expedited NEPA Reviews (Other than Through CEs)

In addition to the option of CEs, the NEPA regulations of the Council on Environmental Quality (CEQ) allow for *alternative arrangements* in the event of an emergency.[82] These alternative arrangements do not waive NEPA requirements, but establish an alternative means of fulfilling those requirements for actions necessary to control the immediate impacts of an emergency, typically with conditions on short-term and long-term actions.[83] For example, in 1998, the Forest

---

[80] 68 *Fed. Reg.* 68254 (Dec. 8, 2003).

[81] See CRS Report RL33779, *The Endangered Species Act (ESA) in the 110th Congress: Conflicting Values and Difficult Choices*, by Eugene H. Buck et al.

[82] 40 C.F.R. §1506.11.

[83] See CRS Report RL33104, *NEPA and Hurricane Response, Recovery, and Rebuilding Efforts*, by Linda Luther.

Service requested alternative arrangements for rapid restoration actions following a windstorm that damaged 103,000 acres of national forest land in Texas that contained critical habitat for the endangered red-cockaded woodpecker; CEQ concurred that the situation was an emergency and agreed to alternative arrangements that included subsequent preparation of an EA, limits on tree removal, long-term public involvement, emergency consultation under ESA, and more.

For fuel treatment, NEPA alternative arrangements will rarely provide a means of accelerated action. First, alternative arrangements are not used very often—42 requests were made from 1980 through 2010.[84] Second, alternative arrangements are to be used for emergencies. Fuel conditions in a delineated area might occasionally be an emergency, such as in the wake of a ice storm or a tornado, but fuel levels generally do not constitute an emergency requiring immediate action.

Healthy Forests Restoration Act

The Healthy Forests Restoration Act of 2003 (HFRA; P.L. 108-148, 16 U.S.C. §§6501-6591) expedited review processes in several ways. In Title I, it modifies the NEPA environmental analysis and public involvement processes for authorized Forest Service and BLM fuel reduction projects (based on priorities, exclusions, and other standards in the act). The EA or EIS for each project may be limited to the proposed action, the no-action alternative, and possibly an additional alternative (in contrast to the range of alternatives normally required). The agencies "shall facilitate collaboration" with tribes and state and local governments and "participation" of interested persons; however, the law does not explain the distinction between *collaboration* with certain interests and *participation* by other interests.

Title I includes two other changes to accelerate fuel reduction projects. First, for the Forest Service, it replaces ARA administrative appeals with a "predecisional administrative review process." This process is only available to persons who submitted "specific written comments that relate to the proposed action" during scoping or the public comment period on the draft NEPA document. The process is also limited to the period between completing the EA or EIS and issuing the record of decision, with no requirements for how long that period must be. Then, the act restricts judicial review, generally limiting plaintiffs to those who have exhausted administrative review processes and specifying the venue for review, while encouraging expeditious judicial review and requiring the courts to balance the short- and long-term effects of action and inaction in deciding on injunctions.

In Title IV, HFRA allows the use of CEs for "applied silvicultural assessments"—timber harvesting and other vegetative treatments "for information gathering and research purposes." Each treatment is limited to 1,000 acres, with exclusions for certain areas and limitations on the adjacency of treatments, and with public notice and comment and "peer reviewed by scientific experts selected by the Secretary [of Agriculture or of the Interior], which shall include non-Federal experts." Total acreage of all applied silvicultural assessments using this CE is limited to 250,000 acres.

---

[84] Council on Environmental Quality, "Alternative Arrangements" website, http://ceq.hss.doe.gov/nepa_information/ alternative_arrangements.html.

Other Possibilities

Congress can create other means of accelerating the decision-making process for fuel reduction treatments. Congress has exempted certain federal activities (such as construction of the Trans-Alaska Pipeline to deliver oil from the North Slope) from NEPA compliance.[85] Congress has also directed in law that no EIS or EA be prepared in certain instances, through direct statutory language or by deeming that the authorized activities are not major federal actions that significantly affect the human environment. Congress has also pronounced certain analyses or substitute processes to be sufficient or adequate under NEPA.

Congress has also established alternative review processes. Typically this is in addition to NEPA public involvement, to accelerate the review by obtaining broader, organized review early in the decision-making process, vetting the decision before public review. Examples include resource advisory committees (RACs) under Section 403 of the Federal Land Policy and Management Act of 1976 (FLPMA; P.L. 94-579, 43 U.S.C. §1753) and under Title II of the Secure Rural Schools and Community Self-Determination Act of 2000 (P.L. 106-393; 16 U.S.C. §500 note). Other advisory or collaborative groups have been established or acknowledged statutorily, commonly to provide supplemental public involvement.

Considerations in Expediting Decisions

Public acceptance of options to accelerate fuel treatments depends on a variety of factors. In general, earlier discourse among interests about the risks and needed treatments lead to greater comfort with the resulting decisions. One study found that survey respondents were willing to accept limitations on the rights to appeal and litigate agency decisions, but wanted to be more informed and involved in those decisions.[86] Greater specificity in approved treatments also is likely to result in greater acceptance. For example, a treatment prescription that specifies "thinning from below to approximately 20-foot spacing of remaining trees and emphasizing retention of Ponderosa pine" is likely to be more acceptable than "mechanical treatment to reduce stand density." Finally, authors have identified the need for *collective action* to minimize conflict over decisions, and three broad social factors to achieve collective action: developing collaborative capacity, framing problems in mutually understood terms, and creating mutual trust among groups.[87] These are factors that take time, and cannot be legislated directly, although Congress can foster (or negate) their development by the ways in which it authorizes agency action to promote wildfire protection.

---

[85] See CRS Report 98-417, *Statutory Modifications of the Application of NEPA*, by Pamela Baldwin.

[86] David M. Ostergren, Kimberly A. Lowe, Jesse B. Abrams, and Elizabeth J. Ruther, "Public Perceptions of Forest Management in North Central Arizona: The Paradox of Demanding More Involvement but Allowing Limits to Legal Action," *Journal of Forestry*, v. 104 (Oct./Nov. 2006), pp. 375-382.

[87] Jeffrey J. Brooks, Alexander N. Bujak, Joseph G. Champ, and Daniel R. Williams, *Collaborative Capacity, Problem Framing, and Mutual Trust in Addressing the Wildland Fire Social Problem: An Annotated Reading List*, Gen. Tech. Rept. RMRS-GTR-182 (Ft. Collins, CO: USDA Forest Service, Rocky Mountain Research Station, Nov. 2006).

Conclusions

As more acres and more homes have burned in the past few years, and more people are at risk from wildfires, Congress has faced increasing pressures to protect structures and resources. Congress decides what programs to authorize and fund, and many options exist.

To protect homes, Congress could create new programs and expand existing ones for installing non-flammable roofing, removing burnable materials adjacent to structures, and creating a defensible space of at least 30 feet around the building. Programs could inform homeowners, or assist or require landowner action; the programs could be federal or implemented through state or local governments.

Protecting resources poses different challenges for Congress, because ecological damages vary widely, depending on the ecosystem and on site-specific conditions. Fuel reduction can probably moderate crown fire damages in surface fire ecosystems, and possibly in mixed-intensity fire ecosystems. Existing programs for federal lands authorize prescribed burning (intentional fires under prescribed conditions) and mechanical treatments (cutting and removing some trees), the principal means of reducing fuel levels. However, prescribed fires are risky and mechanical treatments can cause other ecological damages, and both are expensive. Proponents of more fuel treatment advocate accelerated processes for environmental analysis and public review to reduce costs and expedite action. Others caution that inadequate analysis and review can allow projects with unintended damages and few fire protection benefits. Congress can alter the existing environmental and public review processes, recognizing the trade-offs between expeditious action and insufficient review. However, the fact is that crown fires occur; they cannot be halted and the damages they cause cannot be totally prevented.

Appendix. Excerpts from Forest Service Handbook on NEPA Categorical Exclusions Related to Structural or Resource Protection From Wildfires

The following materials are excerpts from the Forest Service handbook on NEPA categorical exclusions—*FSH 1909.15—Environmental Policy and Procedures Handbook. Chapter 30—Categorical Exclusion from Documentation*, Amendment No. 1909.15-2007-1 (February 15, 2007). Emphases (underscoring and boldface font) are in the original.

30.3 - Policy

...

2. Resource conditions that should be considered in determining whether extraordinary circumstances related to the proposed action warrant further analysis and documentation in an EA or EIS are:

   a. Federally listed threatened or endangered species or designated critical habitat, species proposed for Federal listing or proposed critical habitat, or Forest Service sensitive species.

   b. Flood plains, wetlands, or municipal watersheds.

   c. Congressionally designated areas, such as wilderness, wilderness study areas, or national recreation areas.

   d. Inventoried roadless areas.

   e. Research natural areas.

   f. American Indians or Alaska Native religious or cultural sites.

   g. Archaeological sites, or historic properties or areas.

...

31.2 - Categories of Actions for Which a Project or Case File and Decision Memo Are Required

...

6. *Timber stand and/or wildlife habitat improvement activities which do not include the use of herbicides or do not require more than one mile of low standard road construction....* Examples include but are not limited to: ...

   b. Thinning or brush control to improve growth or to reduce fire hazard including the opening of an existing road to a dense timber stand.

   c. Prescribed burning to control understory hardwoods in stands of southern pine.

d. Prescribed burning to reduce natural fuel build-up and improve plant vigor.

...

10. *Hazardous fuels reduction activities using prescribed fire, not to exceed 4,500 acres, and mechanical methods for crushing, piling, thinning, pruning, cutting, chipping, mulching, and mowing, not to exceed 1,000 acres.* Such activities:

a. Shall be limited to areas:

(1) In the wildland-urban interface; or

(2) Condition Classes 2 or 3 [moderate or high risk of ecological damage] in Fire Regimes I, II, or III [surface fire, stand-replacement fire at 35 years or less, and mixed-intensity fire], outside the wildland-urban interface;

b. Shall be identified through a collaborative framework as described in "A Collaborative Approach for Reducing Wildland Fire Risks to Communities and Environment 10-Year Comprehensive Strategy Implementation Plan";

c. Shall be conducted consistent with agency and Departmental procedures and applicable land and resource management plans;

d. Shall not be conducted in wilderness areas or impair the suitability of wilderness study areas for preservation as wilderness; and

e. Shall not include the use of herbicides or pesticides or the construction of new permanent roads or other new permanent infrastructure; and may include the sale of vegetative material if the primary purpose of the activity is hazardous fuel reduction.

...

12. *Harvest of live trees not to exceed 70 acres, requiring no more than ½ mile of temporary road construction.* Do not use this category for even-aged regeneration harvest or vegetation type conversion. The proposed action may include incidental removal of trees for landings, skid trails, and road clearing. Examples include but are not limited to:

a. Removal of individual trees for sawlogs, specialty products, or fuelwood.

b. Commercial thinning of overstocked stands to achieve the desired stocking level to increase health and vigor.

13. *Salvage of dead and/or dying trees not to exceed 250 acres, requiring no more than ½ mile of temporary road construction.* The proposed action may include incidental removal of live or dead trees for landings, skid trails, and road clearing. Examples include but are not limited to:

a. Harvest of a portion of a stand damaged by a wind or ice event and construction of a short temporary road to access the damaged trees.

b. Harvest of fire-damaged trees.

14. *Commercial and non-commercial sanitation harvest of trees to control insects or disease not to exceed 250 acres, requiring no more than ½ mile of temporary road construction, including removal of infested/infected trees and adjacent live uninfested/uninfected trees as determined necessary to control the spread of insects or disease.* The proposed action may include incidental removal of live or dead trees for landings, skid trails, and road clearing. Examples include but are not limited to:

a. Felling and harvest of trees infested with southern pine beetles and immediately adjacent uninfested trees to control expanding spot infestations.

b. Removal and/or destruction of infested trees affected by a new exotic insect or disease, such as emerald ash borer, Asian long horned beetle, and sudden oak death pathogen.

Author Contact Information

Kelsi Bracmort
Specialist in Agricultural Conservation and Natural
Resources Policy
kbracmort@crs.loc.gov, 7-7283

Acknowledgments

This report was originally written by Ross Gorte, retired CRS Specialist in Natural Resources Policy.